To Franco Locatelli, the lumberjack who plants trees—F. P.

2015 First US edition
Translation copyright © 2015 by Charlesbridge Publishing. Translated by Dominique Clément,
French Cultural Center of Boston.

Published by Charlesbridge
85 Main Street
Watertown, MA 02472
(617) 926-0329
www.charlesbridge.com

First published in France in 2012 by Éditions Rue du monde, 5 rue de Port-Royal,
78960 Voisins-le-Bretonneux, France, as *Wangari Maathai, la femme qui plantait
des millions d'arbres* by Franck Prévot and Aurélia Fronty.
Copyright © 2011 Rue du monde • www.ruedumonde.fr

Library of Congress Cataloging-in-Publication Data
Prévot, Franck, 1968–
  [Wangari Maathai. English]
  Wangari Maathai: the woman who planted millions of trees / by Franck Prévot;
illustrated by Aurélia Fronty. — First US edition.
    pages cm
  ISBN 978-1-58089-626-9 (reinforced for library use)
  ISBN 978-1-60734-795-8 (ebook)
  ISBN 978-1-60734-794-1 (ebook pdf)
1. Maathai, Wangari. 2. Green Belt Movement (Society: Kenya)
3. Environmentalists—Kenya—Biography. I. Fronty, Aurélia. II. Title.
GE56.M33P7413 2015
333.75'153092—dc23
[B]   2013049030

Printed in China
(hc) 10 9 8 7 6 5 4 3 2 1

Display type set in ITC Officina Serif
Text type set in ITC Officina Serif and ITC Officina Sans
Printed by C & C Offset Printing Co. Ltd. in Shenzhen, Guangdong, China
Production supervision by Brian G. Walker
Designed by Martha MacLeod Sikkema

WANGARI MAATHAI

The Woman Who Planted Millions of Trees

Franck Prévot
Illustrated by **Aurélia Fronty**

Charlesbridge

It's almost as if Wangari Maathai is still alive, since the trees she planted still grow. Those who care about the earth as Wangari did can almost hear her speaking the four languages she knew—Kikuyu, Swahili, English, and German—while she carried out her important work with important people.

Wangari encouraged many village women. She dug holes with them in the red soil—holes in which to plant hope for today and forests for tomorrow.

When Wangari planted a large-leafed ebony tree or an African tulip tree, she was reminded of her own roots. She was born in 1940 in the little village of Ihithe, across from the majestic volcano Mount Kenya, which her people consider holy.
This is her story.

The immense forest around Wangari's childhood home is populated by bongo antelopes, monkeys, and butterflies. The leopard, called the *ngari* by Wangari's people, lives here, too. It may be because *wa-ngari* means "she who belongs to the leopard" that Wangari feels as though she is part of the entire forest.

Wangari fetches water every day at the foot of the big *mugumo*, the generous fig tree. As the eldest sister of five siblings, she is the second lady of the house. She helps her mother with countless tasks: gathering wood for the fire, cooking, looking after the little children, and doing farm chores.

Wangari's mother gives her a little garden.
Wangari learns to dig and plant. In the shade
of the big *mugumo*, her mother teaches her
that a tree is worth more than its wood, an
expression that Wangari never forgets.

Wangari's father works for Sir Neylan, one of the ruling British colonists. The British claim the best land for themselves and insist that Kenyans take Christian names. As a result, Wangari is called Miriam during her childhood. The British grow richer by cutting trees to plant more tea.

Wangari remembers the first trees she saw fall.

She doesn't yet know that she can change things with her voice and her hands.

One evening in their little house made of mud walls and dried dung, Wangari's big brother Nderitu asks their mother a question: "Why doesn't Wangari go to school?"

Wangari knows the answer. Daughters must help their mothers before getting married and having children of their own.

But without even realizing it, Nderitu changes things by asking his question.

A few days later Wangari is running joyfully to school with her brothers and cousins! She is thankful to Nderitu for daring to ask the right question, and to her mother for making the decision that will change Wangari's life.

Wangari wants to know and understand everything, and going to school helps her succeed. She receives her high-school diploma at a time when very few African women even learn to read.

Senator John F. Kennedy, the future US president, invites six hundred young Kenyans to come to the United States to pursue their studies. Wangari is one of the students.

For the next five years, Wangari discovers snow, forests of skyscrapers, and people who look nothing like her. Even cornfields in America are different from those at home.

Wangari also discovers that even in a great, free, independent country, some places are forbidden to black people. Just like at home, some schools are for white people only. During the 1960s angry African Americans demand the same rights as white people.

At the same time, in faraway Kenya, another anger turns into triumph. For more than ten years, black people have been demanding the right to cultivate their land and govern their own country. Now they achieve independence from Britain at last.

When Wangari returns home, the British colonists are no longer the masters of Kenya. The country is free, but the trees are not—they still cannot grow in peace. Kenyans are cutting down trees and selling them as the colonists did. By using the land where the trees used to grow to cultivate the tea, coffee, and tobacco sought by rich countries, they can make more money.

Wangari travels through the country to study wildlife and is shocked. Wild animals are rare now—they have fled the chain saws. Women can no longer feed their children, since plantations for rich people have replaced food-growing farms. Rivers are muddy—the soil has been washed away by rain because there are no tree roots to hold it back.

Now Wangari knows how she will make use of her studies and the people she has met. She will explain to the world's great leaders and to Kenya's farmers that a forest is one of the most precious treasures of humanity. She'll tell them that planting thousands of trees will help change the lives of men and women—black and white, rich and poor, in Kenya and elsewhere.

Wangari knows that a tree is worth much more than its wood, as her mother taught her. A tree is a treasure that provides shade, fruit, pure air, and nesting places for birds, and that pulses with the vitality of life. Trees are hideouts for insects and provide inspiration for poets. A tree is a little bit of the future.

Wangari wants to shout to the world, but change happens slowly. She doesn't want to wait. So in 1977 she creates the Green Belt Movement in order to start planting trees immediately.

Traveling from village to village, she speaks on behalf of trees, animals, and children. She asks that people think about the future even if the present is harsh and difficult. She encourages villagers to discuss their problems in their own words—in the language of their tribe.

Her words travel to villages, into newspapers, and through letters to the Kenyan government and international organizations. She needs to raise money because replacing hundreds of thousands of missing trees is expensive.

Wangari creates tree nurseries across Kenya which she entrusts to village women. She provides the women with a financial bonus for each tree that grows.

The government officials who built their fortunes by razing forests try to stop Wangari. Who is this woman who confronts them with a confident voice in a country where women are supposed to listen and lower their eyes in men's presence?

Wangari believes confident women have an important role to play in their families, in their villages, and on the entire African continent. She can't be quiet. With countless sisters to help, "she who belongs to the leopard" doesn't get discouraged. She keeps planting forests.

Wangari is determined not to let one more single tree be cut down. She doesn't lower her eyes, even when she faces President Daniel arap Moi, who will rule Kenya for twenty-four years.

He wants to build a sixty-story building and a statue of himself in the heart of Uhuru Park in Nairobi. Wangari rallies her friends to fight the bulldozers, and the project is abandoned.

Moi then plans to launch a huge real-estate project in Karura's forest, which would threaten endangered species such as the blue monkey and the river hog. Wangari stands tall. She calls the world to the rescue, replants trees, and forces the president to back off.

After her victories a Kenyan man tells her: "You are the only man left standing."

But standing up against the authoritarian power of Daniel arap Moi is dangerous. Wangari is now a threat. She knows that the president will stop at nothing to silence her—he is a powerful man who orders police to shoot at crowds of demonstrators.

She is humiliated, hit, hurt, and imprisoned several times, but she doesn't give up. Each time she is released, she fights to liberate political prisoners and speaks out against torture. Wangari receives death threats and often must hide outside of Kenya. But she perseveres.

Wangari wants to make democracy grow—like trees. She knows that if her people work together to decide the laws of her country, it will become stronger.

She dreams that Kenya's children will be able to play with tadpoles in clear water under fig trees at the edge of great forests. She wants them to be able to eat when they are hungry.

Wangari quickly realizes how many more battles she must fight in order to save the trees. She runs several times for elected office, creates an environmental party, and rallies the opposition to try to bring down Daniel arap Moi.

Facing rising protest, President Moi tries to divide the people in order to rule. He knows that when tribes fight one another, the president can quietly govern the way he wants.

Wangari and the Green Belt Movement help foil Moi's trap. She suggests offering young plants from tree nurseries to neighboring tribes in symbolic gestures of peace.

Little by little, those peace trees bear their fruits. Wangari even succeeds in convincing soldiers to help her cultivate friendships among tribes.

President Daniel arap Moi finally falls in 2002. The country has a new constitution, which requires him to retire, and his party loses the election. Wangari is elected to Parliament. The new president appoints her assistant minister of the environment, natural resources, and wildlife.

For Wangari, now affectionately called Mama Miti, or "the mother of trees," a new part of her story begins. She now holds the power to make decisions. She can finally work to make Kenya a fair nation—for women, men . . . and trees!

Today there are more trees in Kenya than there were when Wangari began her work, and democracy has been established. The Green Belt Movement still protects trees, such as those in the Congo Basin, the second-largest tropical forest in the world.

Wangari Maathai and her supporters planted more than thirty million trees. And every day, even now, new ones are planted in Kenya.

Wangari Maathai was awarded the Nobel Peace Prize on October 8, 2004, for the countless seeds of hope she planted and grew over the years. She was the first African woman to receive the prize. To celebrate, she planted a Nandi flame tree at her home in Nyeri, at the base of Mount Kenya.

The mountain and the inhabitants of the forests around it—leopards, bongo antelopes, other wild animals, and humans—must have been proud that day.

Wangari Maathai, Mother of Forests

Despite her numerous responsibilities Wangari Maathai never forgot the importance of the simple and concrete act of planting.

Wendy Stone/Corbis

The Life of Wangari Maathai

Wangari Maathai at a United Nations conference dedicated to human rights

Salvatore di Nolfi/epa/Corbis

• 1884–1885
Gathered in Berlin, European powers set the rules of colonization and extend their areas of influence in Africa.

• 1920
Kenya becomes a colony of the United Kingdom. English colonists who settle there grow crops for export. The country is ruled exclusively by white people.

• April 1, 1940
Wangari Miriam Muta is born in Ihithe, in Kenya's Nyeri District. She is a member of the Kikuyu people. Her father works as a chauffeur for a British colonist in Nakuru, where Wangari lives for four years with her mother, brothers, and sisters before they return to Ihithe in 1947.

• 1948
Thanks to her mother's determination, Wangari enters primary school at a time when very few girls have access to education. The teachers are tough, but she is passionate and learns quickly.

• 1951
At eleven Wangari leaves her family to become a boarding student at Saint Cecilia's Intermediate Primary School, which is run by the Italian nuns of Nyeri. There she must speak only English. Her tribal language, Kikuyu, is forbidden.

• 1952
The Kenyan African National Union (KANU), led by Jomo Kenyatta, launches a violent rebellion against colonial power. In response the British kill, imprison, and torture thousands of Kenyans. A state of emergency is ordered, and Jomo Kenyatta is imprisoned.

Wangari converts to Catholicism and selects Mary Josephine as her new name. She is known as Mary Jo at school.

• 1956
Wangari enters the Girls High School of Loreto near Nairobi. It is run by Irish nuns and reserved for black students.

• 1957
The right to vote is granted to black Kenyans. Eight black people win legislative seats.

• 1959
Wangari receives her high-school diploma.

• 1960
Senator John F. Kennedy (who is elected president later that year) invites six hundred young Kenyans to study in the United States. Wangari is selected and begins her science studies in the United States.

• December 12, 1963
Kenya is officially liberated from colonial rule. A hero of independence, Jomo Kenyatta becomes prime minister and then president.

• 1966
Wangari becomes assistant to the director of the Veterinary Anatomy Department at the University of Nairobi.

• 1967
Wangari continues her studies in Giessen and Munich, Germany.

• 1969
Opposition parties are officially forbidden in Kenya. Wangari marries Mwangi Mathai. They will have three children: Waweru, Wanjira, and Muta.

• 1971
Wangari becomes the first East African woman to earn a PhD. She will be appointed an assistant professor in 1974 and will direct the Department of Veterinary Anatomy at the University of Nairobi starting in 1976.

William Campbell/Sygma/Corbis

Women helping the Green Belt Movement with reforestation in the 1980s

• 1972
The United Nations (UN) creates the United Nations Environment Programme (UNEP) after the first international UN conference on the environment. UNEP widely supports Wangari's efforts.

• 1977
Wangari launches the Green Belt Movement (GBM) to replant trees and fight in favor of women's rights and democracy.

• October 1978
President Jomo Kenyatta dies while in office. The vice president, Daniel arap Moi, is his successor.

• 1979
Wangari's husband asks for a divorce. He refuses to allow her to keep his surname, so she adds an *a* (the Kikuyu spelling) and takes the name Wangari Muta Maathai.

• 1982
Wangari runs for legislative election, but the authorities declare her ineligible. She will run and fail three more times before being elected in 2002.

• 1989
With support, the Green Belt Movement mobilizes against the construction of an office tower in the middle of Nairobi's Uhuru Park and defeats the project.

July 7, 1990
Hundreds of thousands of demonstrators for democracy gather in Kamukunji Park. The police open fire on the crowd, killing several dozen people and wounding hundreds. *Saba saba* (the date, 7/7, in Swahili) will play an important role in the return of democracy to Kenya.

1993
Parliament is suspended. A single-party government is put in place, giving Daniel arap Moi total power. Wangari hides to stay safe but continues to fight, working with the GBM and international supporters.

1997
Wangari creates a new political party, the Mazingira Green Party, and attempts to rally the divided opposition.

2002
Mwai Kibaki succeeds Daniel arap Moi. Wangari is elected a member of Parliament and appointed assistant minister of the environment, natural resources, and wildlife.

2004
Wangari Muta Maathai receives the Nobel Peace Prize "for her contribution to sustainable development, democracy, and peace." She is the first African woman to receive this distinction.

September 25, 2011
Wangari Muta Maathai dies in Nairobi.

Students, after protesting against deforestation and the corrupt ministers who authorized it, are arrested in 1999.

Simon Maina/AFP

Wangari Maathai celebrates with friends the day her Nobel Peace Prize is announced.

Joseph Mathenge/Gamma

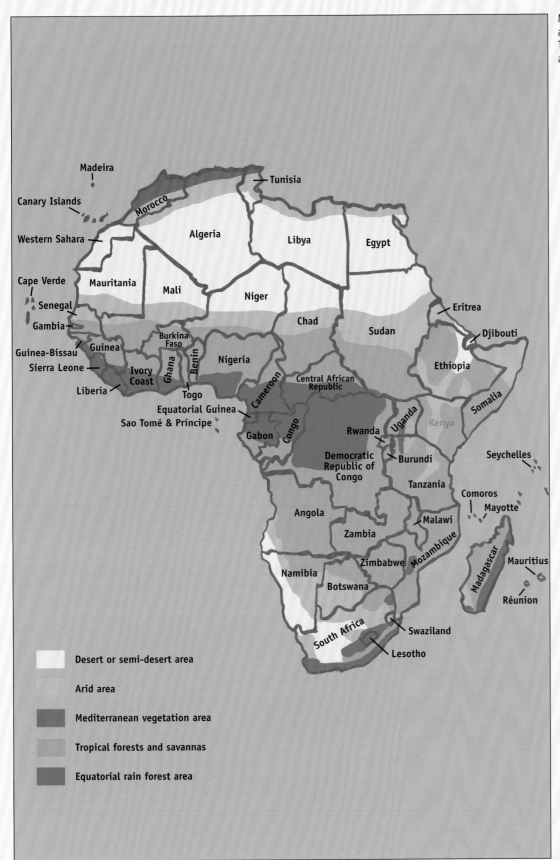

Map of the types of climates and vegetation in Africa. The borders of Kenya appear in red.

Legend:

- Desert or semi-desert area
- Arid area
- Mediterranean vegetation area
- Tropical forests and savannas
- Equatorial rain forest area

Kenya Today

The Republic of Kenya is a country in East Africa located on the coast of the Indian Ocean. Its capital is Nairobi. It has forty-three million inhabitants of diverse ethnic origins. The two official languages are Swahili and English.

The economy of the country is still very fragile. Kenyans cultivate basic agricultural commodities and raise cattle but must import numerous products. Revenue from the sale of exports such as tea, coffee, and cut flowers and from tourism of animal parks is not sufficient to balance the budget.

As is the case almost everywhere in Africa, health is a major issue. The AIDS pandemic and malaria claim many lives each year, especially among the poorest populations.

More than half of Kenyans live below the poverty level. Life expectancy is only fifty-seven years.

43

The Forest: A Treasure in Danger

The bongo is the largest antelope in the world. It is threatened with extinction due to deforestation. Fewer than one hundred are left in the forests of Kenya.

Forests are home to 80 percent of the earth's animal and plant species. And they are being destroyed at an alarming rate.

With only ten billion acres (four billion hectares) left today, forests now cover only 64 percent of the area they covered thousands of years ago. If the current rate of deforestation were to continue, the earth's forests would be gone in two hundred years.

A quarter of the planet's tropical forest is located in Africa, but ten million acres (four million hectares) are destroyed there each year by large corporations that sell the precious wood.

In Kenya forests now occupy about 2 percent of the total land area—compared to approximately 10 percent in 1900. Despite the efforts of the Green Belt Movement and the government, Kenya still loses around 125 thousand acres (50 thousand hectares) of forest each year.

In 2006 the United Nations Environmental Programme launched the Billion Tree Campaign (BTC) sponsored by Wangari Maathai. More than twelve billion trees have been planted in connection with the campaign so far, but the fate of the forests remains worrisome in relation to biodiversity, climate change, and the future of the populations that need forests to survive.

Nigel Pavitt/JAI/Corbis

Stuart Franklin/Magnum

The taking of wood from unmanaged forests wreaks havoc across Africa, South America, and Asia. This photograph shows the transport of logs on a river in Nigeria.

Wangari's Words

Quotations from *Unbowed*, Wangari Maathai's Autobiography

"If you don't foresee the danger and see only the solution, then you can defy anyone and appear strong and fearless." (p. 272)

"As my people would traditionally say: *Arokama kuuraga,* 'May she sleep where it rains.' For me, that place is wet with morning dew and is therefore green. Well, perhaps heaven is green." (p. 276)

"Trees are living symbols of peace and hope." (p. 293)

"A tree . . . tells us that in order to aspire we need to be grounded, and that no matter how high we go it is from our roots that we draw sustenance." (p. 293)

Quotations from Wangari Maathai's Nobel Lecture

"My inspiration partly comes from my childhood experiences and observations of nature in rural Kenya. It has been influenced and nurtured by the formal education I was privileged to receive."

"I would like to call on young people to commit themselves to activities that contribute toward achieving their long-term dreams. They have the energy and creativity to shape a sustainable future. To the young people I say, you are a gift to your communities and indeed the world. You are our hope and our future."

Wangari Maathai and Nelson Mandela on the day of her Nobel Peace Prize speech

Alexander Joe/AFP

BIBLIOGRAPHY

Maathai, Wangari. *The Challenge for Africa.* New York: Pantheon, 2009.

———. *The Green Belt Movement: Sharing the Approach and Experience.* New York: Lantern Books, 2003.

———. *Unbowed: A Memoir.* New York: Knopf, 2006.

WEBSITES

Green Belt Movement
www.greenbeltmovement.org

UNESCO
www.unesco.org

United Nations
www.un.org

United Nations Environmental Programme
www.unep.org

45